Luca Andrea Giordano

Musical Realism in Puccini's La Bohème

Published by New Generation Publishing in 2012

Copyright © Luca Andrea Giordano 2012

First Edition

The author asserts the moral right under the Copyright, Designs and Patents Act 1988 to be identified as the author of this work.

All Rights reserved. No part of this publication may be reproduced, stored in a retrieval system or transmitted, in any form or by any means without the prior consent of the author, nor be otherwise circulated in any form of binding or cover other than that which it is published and without a similar condition being imposed on the subsequent purchaser.

www.newgeneration-publishing.com

 New Generation Publishing

Inspiration is an awakening, a quickening of all man's faculties, and it is manifested in all high artistic achievements.

Giacomo Puccini

Table of contents

5   Introduction

12   *La Bohème*: a work in progress

22   Dramatic structure

35   Real life drama as art

43   Musical analysis

96   Bibliography

Introduction

The music world at the end of the eighteenth century began to change through Wagner until Verdi. This led to the renewal of "traditional" Italian opera. Under the narrative aspect, it was held together by two cornerstones: the Recitative and the Aria. The former had the duty to accomplish the plot sparking off the dramatic action; the latter, embellished by a virtuoso display through the cabaletta, stopped the time in a kind of lyric oasis moulded *in belcanto* style.

This structure, from the point of view of the *Verismo*, was unacceptable due to its dynamics, suspensions and resumptions. Both Wagner and Verdi eliminated this stern division in "closed form", conferring to the opera a coherent unity (*Durchkomponiert*) in which the word, the sound and the action would have been wisely blended in a total art form delineated by the utmost expressive skills (*Wort-Ton-Drama*).

The musicians of the generation 1860-70, labelled as *Giovane Scuola*, drew on this innovative musical legacy. The most important names to remember in this context are: Giacomo Puccini, Pietro Mascagni, Ruggero Leoncavallo, Umberto Giordano, Francesco Cilea and Alberto Franchetti. Some also include Lorenzo Perosi, even though he wrote only sacred music. The success of these musicians coincided with the growth of an artistic and literary movement known as *Scapigliatura* – a restless, odd and eccentric way of living – putting itself against bourgeois society and its followers with a protest stance. The most passionate supporters – among which Arrighi, the Boito brothers, Dossi and Praga – in fact lashed out either against Italian Romanticism, considered too languid and extroverted, or against provincialism of the Risorgimento culture, looking at reality in a different way, trying to individuate the subtle relationship between physical and psychic aspects.

Hence it derives the charm that the theme of illness exerted on their poetics as well as on the French Bohemians', which often tragically affected their own short lives.

The common denominator of these personalities is the development of that dualistic conscience which emphasized the striking contrast between the "ideal" that one would achieve and the "true", the raw reality, described in an objective and anatomic way. As a result, one can perceive the appeal to the typically German models, by E.T.A. Hoffmann, Jean Paul, Heinrich Heine and French, Charles Baudelaire in particular.

The merits of this movement are various. Above all, its position in the cultural history of the nineteenth century is a sort of intellectual crossroad, through which trends of thoughts, forms of foreign literature and literary themes filter through and contribute to renewing and removing the air of provincialism from the Italian cultural climate. Secondly, it purified the language from an obsolete lexicon, fortifying the dramatic conflict without belittling the poetical value of the text. It has also influenced the *Verismo* in the formulation of its doctrine.

From this point of view, the *Verismo* is a literary trend developing towards the end of 1800s and the beginning of 1900s, inspired by the French Naturalism of Émile Zola who, in turn, relates to the thesis by biologist Claude Bernard and the historian Ippolito Taine. These cultural expressions, in respect to the application of the methods of natural and social science, offer to tell human stories in their inner objectivity without altering reality.

To translate into literary terms this conception of life caught in personal experiences, contributes the «impersonality» that is the duty of the writer to detach himself from the context he has created, thus avoiding the betrayal of his feelings and leaving each single development to the work itself.

Another distinctive feature is the so called "concept of the oyster", based on the belief that for the underprivileged it is necessary to stay close to family values, one's work, and ancient traditions in order to avoid the "voracious fish", that is the world, from devouring them. The themes deal with the problems of social life and folklore; that is why many works make use of dialect as a vehicle of communication. Among the greatest exponents we remember Giovanni Verga, Luigi Capuana and Grazia Deledda.

By virtue of this, the protagonists of the works created by the *Giovane scuola* are human beings with their defects and weaknesses so that the public can easily identify with them. The unity of action can be considered the fulcrum of these compositions which imply a solid logical process; it is about the sudden mechanism of the so called «*tranche de vie*» that allows the spectator to live step by step the events of history as a witness. There is no lack of criticism! What mainly worries is only the way the *coup de théâtre* is conceived and used as a cold and sudden revelation of this bitter reality; the shiver in fact, comes from the exasperation of the formula of the *tranche de vie* caught in the most violent and bloody aspects. This attitude, on the other hand, defines that theatrical tradition known under the name of *Grand-guignol*.

The intention the *Verismo* had, probably, was not welcomed by the cited musicians as ideological support but instead like a trend of the time. Nevertheless each work of art assimilates the peculiarities of its own time and absorbs the leading concepts.

The new idea of music perceived by Verismo followers, in reality, has the primary purpose to communicate an idea, a state, and/or a value.

How music could represent a place, an image, a climate condition or, more, feelings of joy, sorrow, hate, regret, fear, sadness, love and even the death tie? The answer to this enigma is completely contained in the project of the artistic path of the *Verismo* consisting in the creation of works as a total and multiform expression of the image as well as an extension of the word.

Let us observe, once and for all, Mascagni in his famous opera *La cavalleria rusticana*: he puts forward the dialect of the word, along with the "music dialect" – proposing those typical themes which represent the southern Italian music culture – and certain melodic inflections expressly recalling a local event. Besides, let us notice the active presence of the people, no more a simple choir limited to commenting on the action but a mass, completing and colouring the action.

The same function of the people can be found at the beginning of Scene II of *La Bohème* by Puccini, where the crowd sings, shouts, runs and lives.

Furthermore, the outline of the expression, in *Verismo* music, is accompanied by a series of objects that refine the scene in order to convey everyday realism in the best possible way.

As a result of this, for instance, we can cite some objects used by Puccini to complete the scenic and music action: the mermaid of the barge at the beginning of *Il Tabarro*, the great bell in St. Peter's Basilica in *Tosca*, the glasses in the III scene of *La Bohème*, the laces in *Manon Lescaut*.

It is, in any case, about "instruments" producing noises – conferring a new semiotic key of reading – which are considered as part of the score with the same importance of those produced by the orchestra... it has to do with the instruments staging everyday noises, the ones well known and foregone that, wisely moulded in the scene, become real, new, surprising and touching.

LA BOHÈME: A WORK IN PROGRESS

The composition of a magnificent opera like *La Bohème*, required the collaboration of three rare talented artists, which resulted in a happy marriage of creativity and genius! It is not a case that Giacomo Puccini – mind and driving force of the sublime achievement – availed himself of the faithful and commendable support of Luigi Illica and Giuseppe Giacosa. It was from the above-mentioned two librettists that the composer from Lucca obtained his best librettos (*La Bohème, Tosca, Madama Butterfly*), so that even after Giacosa's death he tried to re-create a "threesome collaboration".[1]
The artistic approach of Illica – who had an excellent skill as a scriptwriter and dramatist – and Giacosa – appreciated for his poetical abilities, the refined style and the metric mastery – was the ideal combi-

---

[1] In all the operas subsequent *Madama Butterfly* Puccini availed himself of at least two collaborators; the unique exceptions were *Gianni Schicchi* and *Suor Angelica* by Forzano.

nation to let Puccini accomplish the creation of an authentic masterpiece.

Nevertheless, the explosive inventiveness of the musician needed to find a sort of symbiosis with his two librettists' work; this led to the orderliness of his project.

The priority went to the dramatic scheme on which Puccini based the first musical ideas, in their turn responsible to provide a cue – as shown in the following illustration – for versification:

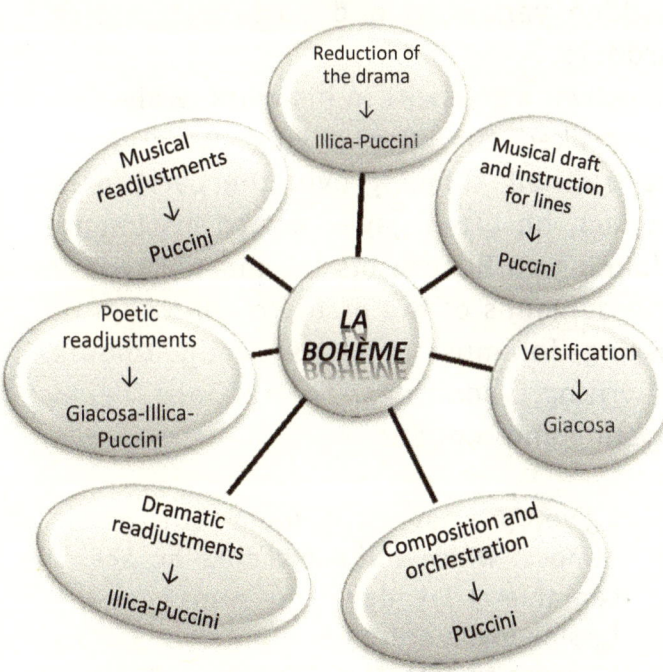

Puccini gave high value to poetry and very often he used to ask his collaborators to modify the lines and their disposition or the metrics according to his musical needs. Illica did not always accept these situations placidly but tried – at least at the beginning of the cooperation, even if in vain – to assert his point of view with the publisher Giulio Ricordi. Afterwards, both librettists accustomed themselves to the composer's tempers, resigned to his sudden variations and particular musical ardours.

Illica was very swift in his work, while Giacosa liked to write paying attention to each detail, thinking over the particulars. In fact, he often gave vent to his unease claiming to Ricordi his incompatibility with the demands of the maestro, who kept on asking, for musical needs, readjustments, rewriting, additions, corrections, cuts, pasting and reductions:

> I give up. I have sent you a little, my utmost, which I think should be acceptable. I lay down my arms, confessing my impotence.
> (Giacosa to Ricordi, 6th October 1893)

To the consequent request of Giacosa to resign his commitment, the publisher extended to playing for him, in a kind of preview, most of the score, trying to persuade him that his efforts were not in vain being a sensible contribution to such a great artistic issue. It was just listening to the music that convinced the dramatist, who in *La Bohème* made his debut as a librettist, not to desist from his work. On the contrary he felt more motivated, conscious of what his poetry had contributed to giving rise to:

> Puccini has exceeded all my expectations! ... and I now understand his tyranny of lines and accents.
> (Giacosa to Ricordi, 20th June 1895)

Ricordi keeps watching everything about the way his maestros operate; he treasures every quality, strength and art with respect and fondness, as witnessed in a fragment of a letter addressed to Illica:

> [...] We all have a peaceful conscience; we have worked heartily, without any bias, serenely enshrouded in the pure atmosphere of art: sor-

ry if I say "we" and not "they". It seems to me that this wonderful Bohème is, if not a little my daughter, at least a bit my goddaughter.
(Ricordi to Illica, February 15th 1896)

Searching for a subject on which to develop his opera, Puccini did not perceive the way for a winning solution, being on the one hand attracted by an exotic story – as *Lakmé* by Léo Delibes – and on the other, being interested in an adaptation of *La lupa* by Giovanni Verga, the father of the *Verismo*, which had inspired the subject of the triumphal *La cavalleria rusticana* by Pietro Mascagni in 1890.

In spite of this, the musician soon aimed towards a novel issued in 1851, *Scènes de la Bohème*,[2] by Henry Murger,[3] that being

---

[2] *Scènes de la Bohème* by Murger is the novel that the publisher Levy presented in 1851, grouping together the numerous episodes of *Scènes de bohème,* issued in instalments in the Parisian review *Le Corsaire*, from March 1845 to April 1849. The title was acquired at the third edition, in 1852, translated by Felice Camerone and published in 1872 by Sonzogno, to be later reprinted in 1890.

not subjected to copyright, could be used as source of inspiration for a functional libretto.[4]

---

[3] Previously, the literary narration had a great success, so that the dramatist Theodore Barriere, together with Murger, connected some of these brief episodes gaining a structure in five acts, *La vie de Bohème*, staged on November, 22nd 1849 at the Théâtre des Variétés in the presence of Louis-Napoléon Bonaparte, Theophile Gautier and the most famous representatives of the Parisian literary world of those days.

[4] Murger also inspired another Italian operatic composer, Ruggero Leoncavallo. This transpired as a result of defiance, competition, a little bit of jealousy and some disloyalty. It seems that Puccini's excitement arose soon after the première of *Manon Lescaut* (1st February 1893). Indeed Puccini himself expressed his thoughts to lawyer Carlo Nasi and to a journalist during a train ride from Turin to Milan on the occasion of the debut of Verdi's last opera, *Falstaff*. Nasi himself proposed to set out the scenes while the journalist would have written the libretto: in a nutshell, the genesis arose as a joke but already at this early planning stage the division of the roles appeared clear. As chance would have it, however, Puccini and Leoncavallo met some time later at the Gallery De Cristoforis in Milan. The two composers realized that their works coincided; Leoncavallo too was ready

to produce the music for his *La Bohème* and his anger can be easily understood. In actual fact, the musician went right away to Edoardo Sonzogno, his editor as well as to the impresario of La Scala, in order to agree upon an advertising strategy to let people know he had priority in this project. It would have been enough to open a newspaper by chance, in 1893, to realize this. In fact, *Il Secolo* announced the forthcoming issue of the new opera by the brilliant composer of *I Pagliacci*, while *Il Corriere della Sera* was more detailed since it highlighted how Leoncavallo had been working at *La Bohème* for some months, proposing to première it in 1894, while Puccini, on the contrary, had been interested in the subject for only a few days. The debate was rather evident, but Puccini did not think of standing up for himself to retort the "charges". Besides, the two composers had harbored a mutual fondness and friendship for each other since some time. However, Puccini hinted at having no more time for a rethink, though his intention was not to cause offence to his friend. Some sentences of his letter are illustrative about what it was about to be: *If he sets to music, I will set to music. The public will judge. The priority in art does not imply that one has to render the same subject with the same artistic intent.* Even Jules Massenet thought of joining as the third wheel, but that urge suddenly faded. The challenge had to occur between the pro-

Puccini and his librettists ran up against a difficult work! It was necessary to obtain from an episodic story, an operatic storyline which had to be essential, consistent,

---

tagonists and the story line. Why? First and foremost, Puccini was able to finish the opera before Leoncavallo, so that the two premières differed by fifteen months (1st February 1896 the former, 6th May 1897 the latter). If the truth be told, Leoncavallo gained the upper hand initially, even if this predominance did not last long. Actually, in Puccini's opera there are a lot of emotions but also their control, a well measured blend of happiness and sadness. Leoncavallo instead aimed at his literary culture and to a greater number of characters. From this point of view, therefore, there are some scenes whose absence would not cause any astonishment. Moreover, a lacuna in Leoncavallo's work is the excessive cheerfulness and euphoria in the first part of the opera, while melancholy dominates the second. Puccini, instead, has measured out with a greater care those so conflicting moods. Finally, Leoncavallo himself was not able to organize a valuable work in order to clearly distinguish one act from another one; Puccini has adapted this system and has been able to shape each scene to the sentimental changes of the characters.

and at the same time faithful to the spirit of the novel.

Illica, first and foremost, had to reduce the high number of roles, banning some characters present in Murger's novel, among which included the various love affairs of Rodolphe (the *grisette*[5] Louise, the starlet Sidonie, the milliner Laure, Seraphine, Juliette).

The most extreme and complex resolution was the change of *mademoiselle Lucille*, said Mimì - in the novel presented as Rodolphe's unfaithful and spiteful bride - into the romantic maiden we all know.

The librettist was also careful about the tiniest details, such as the name of the magazine of which Rodolfo was the copy editor, *Le Castor*; *Cafè Momus*, the group's meeting point; the title of Marcello's painting, *Le passage de la mer Rouge*; the newspaper that Rodolfo took out his pocket to 'set the table' once Schaunard

---

[5] A French term for a girl or young married woman of the lower class as well as a young working-class woman of perceived easy morals. The term refers to the grey (*gris* in French) fabric used for dresses.

had entered carrying food supplies, bottles of wine, cigars and a firewood bundle, the *'Costituzional'* (reference to *Le Constitutionnel*, a French political and literary newspaper, founded in Paris during the Hundred Days by Joseph Fouché).

Among the particulars excerpted from the chapters of the novel, those of the candle blown out by a breath of wind (from *Le manchon de Francine*, chap. XVIII), the loss of the key and the muff to warm the ill woman's cold hands stand out.

Therefore, the merit of the dramatic reduction of the *Scenès* is attributed to Illica. The effective realization of the opera was a result of the outline initially prepared, with all its elements successfully interwoven, by hard work.

DRAMATIC STRUCTURE

According to German novelist and playwright Gustav Freytag (1816 - 1895), a drama is divided into five parts which some refer to as a dramatic arc: rising, climax, falling action, and dénouement.

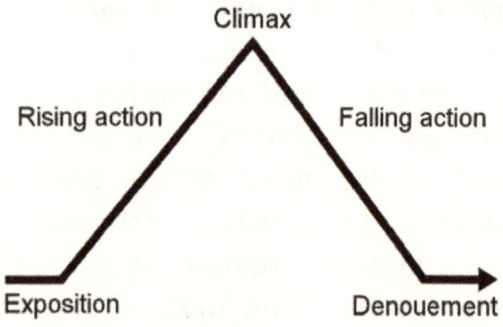

- EXPOSITION. It introduces important background information to the audience;
- RISING ACTION. It is about a related series of incidents built toward the point of greatest interest;
- CLIMAX. It is the turning point, which marks a change, for better or worse, in the protagonist's affairs. If the story is a comedy, things will have gone badly for the protagonist up to this point; now, the plot will begin to unfold in his or her

favour, often requiring the protagonist to draw on one's inner strengths. If the story is a tragedy, the opposite state of affairs will ensue, with things going from good to bad for the protagonist, often revealing the protagonist's hidden weaknesses;
- FALLING ACTION. Here the conflict between the protagonist and the antagonist unravels, with the protagonist winning or losing against the antagonist. The falling action may contain a moment of final suspense, in which the final outcome of the conflict is in doubt;
- DENOUEMENT (also Resolution, or Catastrophe – from old French *desnouer*, "to untie", from *nodus* → Latin for "knot"). It is the unraveling or untying of the complexities of a plot and comprises events from the end of the falling action to the actual ending scene of the drama or narrative. Conflicts are resolved, creating normality for the characters and a sense of catharsis, or release of tension and anxiety, for the reader. The comedy ends with a *dénouement* (a conclusion) in which the protagonist is better off than at the story's outset. The tragedy ends

with a catastrophe in which the protagonist is worse off than at the beginning of the narrative.

According to Freytag's analysis – initially intended to be applied to ancient Greek and Shakespearean dramas and then increasingly used for modern and contemporary works – this chapter and the following ones will be analysed from this perspective.

The original schedule of *La Bohème* had a different structure when compared to the modern one: Scene I was divided into two, titled *In soffitta* [In the garret] and *Al quartiere latino* [At the Latin Quartier]; the second envisaged *La barriera d'Enfer* (At the toll gate – later the actual Scene III); the last scene was *In soffitta* again.

Between *La barriera d'Enfer* and *La soffitta* of act IV, there was a third act titled *Il cortile della casa di via La Bruyère 8* [The courtyard of the house on 8, La Bruyère]. There the two librettists had set a great ball party given by Musetta in the courtyard of her house because she had been evicted by her patron. In this context Mimì and Rodolfo's farewell is introduced.

In the same circle, the Viscount Paolo (who in the opera is only mentioned in the cues of Rodolfo in the Scene III - "*Un moscardino / di Viscontino / le fa l'occhio di triglia*" [A fop of a young Viscount only has to make eyes at her] and Musetta's in the Scene IV - "*Intesi dire che Mimì fuggita / dal Viscontino era in fin di vita*" [I heard someone say that Mimì had left the Viscount, and that she was dying]) gains Mimì's benevolence, causing Rodolfo's furious jealousy. However, this scene was irreparably cut by Puccini, in spite of the contrary opinion of the two librettists. According to the musician, in fact, the introduction of a party at that point of the action would have reproduced the scheme of the *Quartiere latino*, creating a phase of unacceptable reiteration! It was in this way that the two initial scenes were separated, giving rise to the division between the first couple of episodes, dedicated to light-heartedness and love, as well as the two intense closing scenes.

The realization of the opera resulted from a fussy work to which Giulio Ricordi also gave a contribution through his intuitive suggestions. He proposed, for instance, to let Musetta sing off-stage, the waltz she had previously sung at the tables of *Café Momus*; he also suggested that Illica cut the numerous details in order to reduce the plot, thus giving its main feature of essentiality. In spite of the cuts Illica made, his role was decisive in the choices of the dramatic development. In confirmation of this, trying to resolve the problems concerning the scene of the *Quartiere latino*, he prepared a scenic plan;[6] the difficulty of the scenic positions, beyond all doubt, did not have an easy resolution considering that the single episodes – inserted in a mass scenic plot – needed a prominent position in order to grant visibility and understanding.

Illica, therefore, paid a lot of attention to every detail so as to not spoil the credibility of the whole opera. Notwithstanding, once the work was complete, he realized that a particular scene had to be changed because it conflicted with the realistic log-

---

[6] Illica sent Giulio Ricordi the scenic plan together with the draft of a remake of a libretto requested by Puccini, *'... onde isolare i bohèmes'* [... in order to isolate the Bohemians], dated back on January 5th, 1894.

ic core: in Scene II, in fact, the bright group sits at the outer tables of the Coffee Bar, despite the cold of Christmas Eve. The skilful dramatist is compensated for this disagreement of realism, thus making a caption to the libretto:

> Marcello, Schaunard and Colline enter the Café Momus, but leave straight away because they are annoyed by the great and noisy crowd packed inside there. They brought out a table followed by a waiter surprised at their oddity to have dinner outside [...].
>
> With enemies and critics in bad faith on the day, our attitude to be pleased is a little naïve, believe me! And leaving the Bohemians sat at the table dining for almost an act without justifying this in the libretto, believe me, it is a great weapon so that those men do not use it [...].
> (Illica to G. Ricordi, December 7th 1895)

Illica was very resolute to propose the variation of Puccini's first idea about the last scene of *La Bohème*; the reasons, that can help us to understand such steadiness, were expressed in a letter to Ricordi:

> [..] with Mimì in bed, Rodolfo at the desk writing and a candle end to light the scene. That is no separation (after the third scene) between Rodolfo and Mimì! Now not only is there not La Bohème, but, there is no longer Murger's Mimì! Now I say that it is already a mistake that Rodolfo and Mimì's parting does not happen before the very public eye (due to the abolition of Via La Bruyère scene), let us imagine if it did not happen in no other way! The essence of Murger's book is exactly in that freedom of love (supreme peculiarity of La Bohème) through which all the characters act. Think about how great and really touching Mimì can be, who goes dying to the bleak and cold attic room, in Rodolfo's arms. The same Mimì who was able to live with a lover (the Viscount Paolo) offering her some silk and velvet, the one who felt that the tuberculosis was kill-

ing her.[7] It seems impossible to me that Puccini did not feel like understanding its greatness.
(Illica to Ricordi, February 1894)

Once it was noticed that Illica's remarks were right — after numerous, strict elaborations and changes — in 1895 the libretto, polished and perfected by Giacosa, finally assumed its almost complete structure. In the meanwhile Puccini was about to finish the orchestration.

The final result which made *La Bohème* stand apart, everlasting through the following decades, charming and touching

---

[7] In the past, the *Mycobacterium tuberculosis* had also been named "subtle evil" or consumption since it seemed to consume people from inside, with coughing, bleeding from the mouth, fever, pale complexion, reddened and puffy eyes (and consequent sensitiveness to intense light). This infectious disease — sometimes associated with vampirism in ancient lore — was romanticized in the XIX century. Many people believed that tuberculosis caused a state of euphoria defined as *Spesphtisica*, or "hope of the consumed person". It was believed that TB victims had an outburst of creativity while the disease progressed.

for the past and present public, does not let out the long, hard but loving "threesome" work.

It is only his love for this opera, and for its intrinsic meaning, that led Puccini to long for singers who would be able to create on stage – at the première – that special sympathy for the *bohèmiens*. Everything had to contribute to communicate that sense of reality, so hard to obtain during the drafting of the dramatic action; each detail had to reach the spectator's heart and stay there indelible due to its disarming reality!

The distressing aspect of everyday life, experienced with the gracefulness of those who can catch the magic of the little things and learn to navigate without sails and oars, could only be expressed by professional performers who were able to balance voice and dramatic art on stage.

Puccini, on the occasion of the opening night at the Teatro Regio of Turin (February 1st, 1896),[8] so entrusted the roles to

---

[8] The choice of Turin for the opening night did not satisfy Puccini, as witnessed in a sentence of his letter: ' […] first because the theatre is deaf, second for the rule *non bis in idem* [(*lat.* not a

Cesira Ferrani (*Mimì*),[9] Camilla Pasini (*Musetta*), Evan Gorga (*Rodolfo*), Tieste Wilmant (*Marcello*), Michele Mazzara (*Colline*), Antonio Pini-Corsi (*Schaunard*), under the skilful direction of Arturo Toscanini, only twenty years old that time.

La Bohème is recognized as one of the most celebrated and appreciated operas of all time, though critics rapped the première:

> [Puccini cannot be forgiven for] composing his music hurriedly and with very little effort to select and polish..
> ... [The work contains] music that can delight but rarely move. [...] Even the Finale of the opera, so intensely dramatic in situation, seems to me defi-

---

second opera until the success of the previous one) referring to the première of *Manon Lescaut*], third too close to the Milanese people [where, presumably, Sonzogno's partisans would be out in force]. [...] I am not at all pleased that the première will be held in Turin, no way!' (Puccini to Ricordi, October 1895).

[9] The day after the première, Puccini gave her his picture with dedication: «To my real and wonderful Mimì, Miss Cesira Ferrani, with gratitude G. Puccini».

cient in musical form and colour. [...] La Bohème, even as it leaves little impression on the minds of the audience, will leave no great trace upon the history of our lyric theater, and it will be well if the composer returns to the straight road of art, persuading himself that this has been a brief deviation.
(Carlo Bersezio, *Gazzetta piemontese*)

We wonder what could have started Puccini toward the degradation of this *Bohème*. The question is a bitter one, and we do not ask it without a pang, we who applauded and shall continue to applaud [his last opera], in which was revealed a composer who could combine masterly orchestration with a conception in keeping with the best spirit of Italy. [...] You are young and strong, Puccini; you have talent, culture, and imaginative ability such as few possess: you have today conceived the whim of forcing the public to applaud you where and when you will. That is all very well for once, but for once only. For the future, turn back to the great and difficult battles of art.
(Edoardo Augusto Berta, *Gazzetta del Popolo*)

The theatrical agent Carlo D'Ormeville, decreed the future of this opera in a memorable telegram affirming:

> Bohème, a failed opera that will not tour.

But the thesis was soon retracted: Puccini had created in *La Bohème* a dreamy world expressing profound emotions; he allowed the public to identify itself with the characters just like he did. It was an opera he felt as "sensed" on his skin in all colours and nuances: the four young bohemians represent the young artist sharing an attic and fostering their dreams. Puccini too had shared a room with Mascagni; he had lived the real life of a bohemian in the cabins on the shores of lake Massaciuccoli with his usual friends; he too had pawned his coat like Colline.

Mimì, the sweet maiden involved in an unhappy destiny, is expressed by Puccini in her sensitive human nature, in her delicate passion as well as in her profound agony.

In other words, Puccini had translated musically the fleeting dimension of time and youth in this milieu of dreams and frailty, instilling

the opera with the necessary requisites to become great.
And so it was! After the performance in Manchester, *The Times* relates:

> The melody, of a rare facility, is scattered profusely in Puccini's score and often, as in the beautiful scenes between Mimì and Rodolfo, the composer gets unique dramatic effects through relatively simple means.

Manchester was followed by Glasgow, Edinburgh, Paris, Berlin.
The opera had been redeemed by the cold-heartedness of the Regio theatre and launched into the history of the best loved operas all over the world.
So, Carlo Bersezio was wrong: it is just the history of the lyric theatre, instead, to witness the untold greatness of Puccini opera.

REAL LIFE DRAMA AS ART

When the long period of privation was over, thanks to the economic help of his uncle Nicolao Cerù, Puccini finally was able to rent a small house near lake Massaciuccoli, in Torre del Lago,[10] in the prov-

---

[10] Torre del Lago is the home of the Puccini Festival which welcomes about 40.000 spectators every year to its open-air theatre. The festival was established in 1930 following Puccini's wishes: «[...] I always come out here and take a boat to go and shoot snipes [...] but once I would like to come here and listen to one of my operas in the open air». (Puccini in a letter to Giovacchino Forzano in November 1924, before he left for the clinic in Brussels where he died shortly thereafter). The composer expressed his wish to see his creations come to life on the extraordinary natural stage offered by the Massaciuccoli Lake. Forzano was so impressed by those words that, after Puccini's death, he decided to realise that dream. In 1930, together with Pietro Mascagni, who had been a fellow-student and room-mate to Puccini, Forzano began to carry out the first performances of Puccini's operas on the lakeshore, in front of the Maestro's house. On 24th August 1930, in a provisional theatre with the stage built on piles

ince of Lucca (Tuscany). This was the place where the composer used to take refuge from social obligations after his success and where he could devote himself to his music in absolute peace. Close to the lake there was a group of painters belonging to

---

driven into the lake, a travelling opera company performed *La Bohème* directed by Forzano and conducted by Mascagni, with Rosetta Pampanini, Margherita Carosio, Angelo Minghetti and Luigi Montesano. The same travelling company came back to Torre del Lago in 1931: Beniamino Gigli and Adelaide Saraceni performed in *La Bohème*, while Rosetta Pampanini and Angelo Michetti performed in *Madama Butterfly*. One of the world's most famous and beloved opera festivals was born. In 1966 the Festival moved to the reclaimed land just near the small lake harbour. Here the present theatre was built, a large structure enjoying the charming background of the Massaciuccoli Lake with the small villages on the opposite shore, whose flickering lights at night assured an unforgettable natural scenery for the performances taking place on the wide stage. During the over seventy years of the Festival, the stage of Torre del Lago has hosted the most famous and acclaimed names of world opera.

the Macchiaioli,[11] whose aesthetic ideal was closely related to nature and its uncontaminated beauty, just as it appeared in the area of Massaciuccoli at that time, on whose waters reflected the only wood-

---

[11] The pictorial movement of the Macchiaioli developed in Florence between 1800 and 1900. The term was coined in 1862 by an anonymous reviewer of the «*Gazzetta del Popolo*» to define in negative those painters who around 1855 began an anti-academic pictorial movement according the verismo style. At Michelangelo Café, a group of painters who rallied round the critic Diego Martelli gave birth to this movement with the main purpose of renovating Italian pictorial culture. Macchiaioli's artistic expression is based on Verismo principles and stands in the way of Romanticism, Neoclassicism and the academic Purism, claiming that the image of the real is a contrast of areas of light and shadow – or "*macchie*" (literally patches or spots) – initially obtained by a technique called "*dello specchio nero*" [the black mirror], that is making use of a mirror blackened through the smoke, in order to enhance the chiaroscuro contrasts of a painting. These painters' art – as defined by the theorist and critic of the movement, Adriano Cecioni – consisted in «rendering the impressions that they received from life through spots of pale and dark colours».

en cabin – inhabited by fishermen - with the roof made of branches. Puccini was warmly welcomed by the group, and suddenly found a great friend in the painter Ferruccio Pagni.[12] Together with him the musician began to attend the inner circle of friends at Giovanni Gragnani's cabin,[13]

---

[12] Of his surviving works, a few witness a production focused on landscapes – mainly lakes, gloomy and silent atmospheres – as well as a stylistic research addressed to France. In February 1904, after some misunderstandings with Puccini and the estrangement from his Bohemian friends, he decided to move to Argentina. When he came back to Italy between 1917-18, he settled again in Torre del Lago and resumed contact with Puccini and Fanelli. In 1919 he co-founded Club 'Gianni Schicchi' and the 'Accademia degli Zeteti' with Fanelli, Viani, Moses Levy and Puccini; in 1926 he published his Puccini's memoirs.

[13] Giovanni Gragnani nicknamed *Gambe di Merlo* [with legs like a blackbird] by Puccini himself due to the formation of his legs – together with the painters Ferruccio Pagni and Francesco Fanelli - had been a dearest friend and supporter of the composer. Friendship apart, these men had also in common a passion for hunting, good cooking, fishing, table games and some other pleasures. Gragnani was not only a cobbler by trade,

used by himself not only as a home but also as a cobbler's workshop, inn and a meeting-place for his friends. This circle – made of genuine people, objects and circumstances, dedicated to the duty and simple delights of everyday life – certainly influenced Puccini regarding the choice of the subject of *La Bohème*.

This scenario of reality was to the musician a kind of prototype for the inspiration of his dramaturgy: unknown artists, only rich in living love, youth and rejoicing in little pleasures such as a card game, a mouth-watering dish, and some good wine.

When Puccini visited South America, he proposed buying his cabin in order to use

---

second best as a vendor, but also a virtuoso cook. Gambe di Merlo's inn was near Massaciuccoli lake in Torre del Lago. It was a wooden rectangular shaped cabin, a spacious and ventilated place with two big windows without panes and covered in sedge, a typical resource of the marshy area. Its notoriety in Puccini literature is owed to the customers, mainly consisting of intellectuals and notable people of the Italian aristocracy who were close to the musician.

it as *Club La Bohème*, in honour of the opera in progress:

> That opera was a bit ours. Cecco was 'Marcello', me 'Colline', Giacomo, that goes without saying, 'Rodolfo', and the others… 'the happy company'.
> (Ferruccio Pagni)

Naming Cecco, Pagni would refer to Francesco Fanelli, who lived in Torre del Lago with a young widow; their love was quarrelsome, (they often provoked each other as *rospo*, *vipera*, *imbianchino* [toad, viper, whitewasher]) and in their squabbles Puccini probably found the suggestions for the final quartet of the third scene of the opera, sketching out the characters of Marcello and Musetta.

Also, the ironic and playful nature of the group of friends could have inspired the sardonic rebellions of the *bohèmiens* of the opera against the bourgeois society, depicted in the characters of Benoît and Alcindoro. This relationship between the reality lived by Puccini in Torre del Lago and the one staged in *La Bohème* is evidence that the group surely had a prominent role in inspiring the story of the opera:

> That night, while we were playing, Giacomo was at his last bars.[14] - Silence, you guys, - he suddenly said – I have finished! We left the cards, and went close to him. - Now I will let you listen, take your seats again! - This finale is a good one... He attacked from the last melody sung by Mimì: *Sono andati...* As Puccini kept on playing and singing, that music - made of rests, suspensions, light touches, sighs, breathlessness, pervaded by a subtle melancholy and by an intense and profound drama – caught us, and we were able to see the scene and everything, feeling that human torment, since there the expression really has come back to its origins, to its eternal substance: Sorrow. Once the last excruciating chords of the death had fallen, a thrill ran through us and no one was able to choke back their tears. The sweet Mimì lay shivering cold on the meagre cot as the inevitable would silence her tender and kind voice forever.

---

[14] Puccini used to compose surrounded by confusion, a habit also common to Strauss and Mozart.

The vision appeared to us: Rodolfo, Marcello, Schaunard, Colline were our figures or we were their incarnations, Mimì our lover of past days or of a dream, and all that torment was our same torment.
(Ferruccio Pagni)

The friends of the club organized a masked party to solemnize the completion of *La Bohème*; it also was a pretext to greet their dear friend Giacomo, who in December 1895 would have left to Turin where the staging of the opening night was waiting for him.

MUSICAL ANALYSIS

The dramaturgy and the lines of the libretto of *La Bohème* required the music to be in a style of complete naturalness, in order to support an action which lacked static episodes, and to be able to support the lyrical effusions between Rodolfo and Mimì.
In order to avoid being trapped by the customary division of the opera into arias, duets and concertatos – even if keeping within one's own tradition – he recreated a musical setting which was homogeneous and constant. The action of *La Bohème* is tied to everyday life; each situation had to give its prominence to an expression which was simple and high at the same time since a metaphor of a world where time flies off, and whose youth and love pass inexorably under the undeceived eyes of the protagonists.
In the whole opera there is the alternation of ironical moments, love contexts, cheerful atmospheres and tragic situations. The interaction of these several conditions is measured to make these contrasts necessary for the fusion of the plot.

The opera is articulated in four scenes. The first two are characterized by feelings of light-heartedness, playfulness, irony and love. In the third and fourth ones, instead, the feelings of melancholy, sadness, deluded hope, grief and its exacerbation into death have the upper hand.

I scene

In the first scene some motifs will re-occur throughout the opera as a reference to the characters, situations and emotions.

The first theme, in *Allegro vivo*, is that of the *bohème* representing the spirit of the *bohèmien*.

This theme – derived from a juvenile orchestral composition by Puccini, *Capriccio sinfonico* (1883) – has been introduced to link several episodes recurring throughout the opera:

- ✓ IT IS REPRESENTED ALMOST IMMEDIATELY IN THE RECITED SECTION, IN CONJUNCTION WITH THE FALL FROM THE STAIRS

- ✓ THE FIRST THEME OF RODOLFO: "*NEI CIELI BIGI*" [IN THE GREY SKIES]

Rodolfo strikes it up with passion well outlining the fond and ebullient vitality of the poet, as well as his tenderness, trusted to the flutes, when his drama is sacrificed and thrown away in the fireplace to rekindle the fire. While the flutes comment melodically on the action of the poet, the harp recalls the effect of the flames burning the manuscript.

✓ THE THEMES OF COLLINE AND SCHAUNARD

The themes, characterized by horns, introduce the entry of the philosopher Colline and the musician Schaunard.
Entry of Colline:

Entry of Schaunard:

The party atmosphere is interrupted by the coming of the house-owner, Benoît, who comes to collect the rent of the quarter. In this scene too there are some short motifs, as *Alla sua salute!*

[A toast. To your health!] and *Ei gongolava arzillo, pettoruto* [How he swaggered, proud and happy], whence the comic consideration of the bass about his preferences for women is raised. Once Benoît is out of scene, the action goes on quickly until Rodolfo is left alone in the attic.

✓ **THE FIRST ENCOUNTER BETWEEN RODOLFO AND MIMÌ**

Two gentle knocks on the door announce the coming of someone: it is

Mimì, melodically introduced by the theme, which from now on, will be her dreaming theme.

The love encounter between Rodolfo and Mimì, second part of the Scene I, is articulated according to musical sections, each one corresponding to a different climate. With regard to the two solo pieces, Puccini conceived a narrative development proposed in the conversational singing.

✓ *CHE GELIDA MANINA*

In the first section, *Che gelida manina* [How cold your little hand is] introduces a melodic style which is somewhat linear, with rare inflections towards the high register - which does not however impede the linearity of the phrasing.

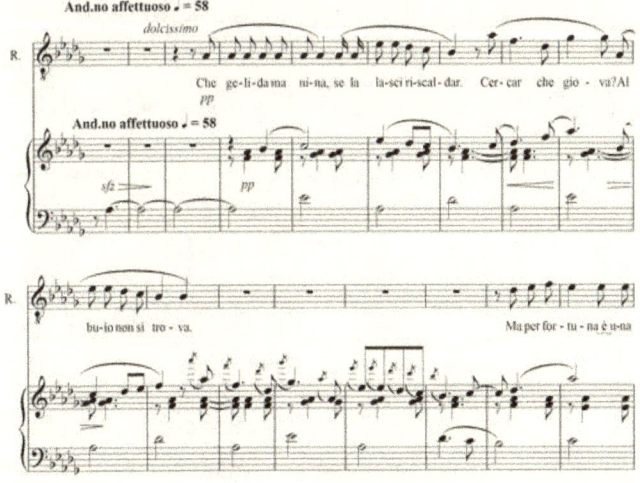

It follows a brief section in the style of the recitative *Chi son?... Chi son?* [Who am I?... Who am I?].

Immediately after, *Nei cieli bigi* [In the grey skies], the first melody of the poet, returns with the words, *In povertà mia lieta* [In my happy poverty].

The ending is the most lyrical, and begins from *Talor dal mio forziere* [Yet sometimes from my safe, all my gems are stolen], in which the high C is part of a tradition that replaces the original A flat.

✓ Sì. Mi chiamano Mimì [Yes, they call me Mimì]

The structure of Mimì's aria, whose initial phrase was anticipated by clarinets at the time that she knocked on the door, is more varied. The melodic element is therefore generated in the orchestra, to then become Mimì's voice and the joining link among the various sections.

This melody becomes a sort of *Leitmotiv* of the protagonist. It follows a section in flowing tone: *La storia mia è breve. Mi piaccion quelle cose* [My story is brief. I delight in these pleasures] begins with a lyric phrasing, emphasized by a *ritardando* on the high A.

The retake of the Leitmotiv is then followed by a conversational section: *Sola mi fo il pranzo da me stessa* [All alone I make myself dinner], up till *ma quando vien lo sgelo* [But when the thaw comes], section of a strong lyric and sentimental effusion revealing Mimì's sensitive soul.

The same theme *Mi piaccion quelle cose* [I delight in these pleasures] arises again in the following phrase *Germoglia in un vaso la rosa* [A rose blossoms in my vase]:

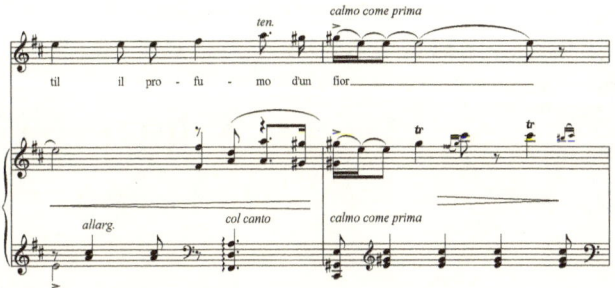

In the same way, an echo of melody is proposed in the two phrases *che parlano di sogni e di chimere* [that talk of dreams and fancies] and *Ma I fior ch'io faccio ahimè!* [But the flowers I make, alas!]: the melodic flowing that is found by observing the two phrases is based on the words *sogni, chimere, fiori* [dreams, fancies, flowers] (that Mimì will define *senza odore* [no scent] in the short), to symbolize – either for the meaning of the words or the descending melody on *chimere* [fancies] and *ahimè* [alas] – the feeling of melancholy and the premonition.

The piece ends with a phrase in recitative style – syllabled in sections of tuplets composed by four, five and ten consequential semiquavers – in order to imitate the spoken word as much as possible.

Scene II

The second scene opens with the Christmas motif of the Latin Quarter, already introduced in the first scene when Schaunard sings *Quando un olezzo di frittelle* [When the smell of fritters]:

The curtain rises showing the vivid crowd, which is none other than the chorus, making its first appearance divided into various groups according to what they represent (sellers, nobles, bourgeois, artists, people). For this scenic pattern, Puccini drew his inspiration from act IV of *Carmen* by Bizet, introducing the mixed chorus and treble chorus, speaking solos through the frantic orchestra. On stage there are a lot of everyday objects.

In the crowd, among the screams of sellers, children and mothers, Mimì and Rodolfo – busy purchasing a pink bonnet – stand out in their love phrasing. In this synergic interaction of music and scenic elements, no episode loses its significance: Schaunard buys a pipe and an off-key horn (*Falso questo re* [That D's out of tune]), Colline fills up the old coat he has just purchased with books, Marcello plays around with women, Rodolfo gives a pink bonnet to Mimì as a present, while the love motif reappears:

The episode of Musetta and her rapprochement to Marcello, unlike the encounter between Rodolfo and Mimì, does not imply the division of the scene into two halves but fits in with the mass scene. From the theme (the score specifies: *fortissimo, brillante con fuoco*) Puccini created the melody that portrays the frivolity of the character, which comes up again in *Voglio fare il mio piacere* [I'm going to do just as I please].

✓ ENTRY OF MUSETTA

A bar before *Voglio fare il mio piacere*:

✓ MUSETTA'S WALTZ

The action stops after few bars when Musetta begins to sing the slow and sensual waltz *Quando me'n vo'…*, [When I walk out alone among the street] whose charming melody Marcello is not able to resist; after the ironic concertato in which the music follows the singing, the painter resumes, doubled by the orchestra at the peak of the volume, in *Gioventù mia* [Youthful desire] waltz time.

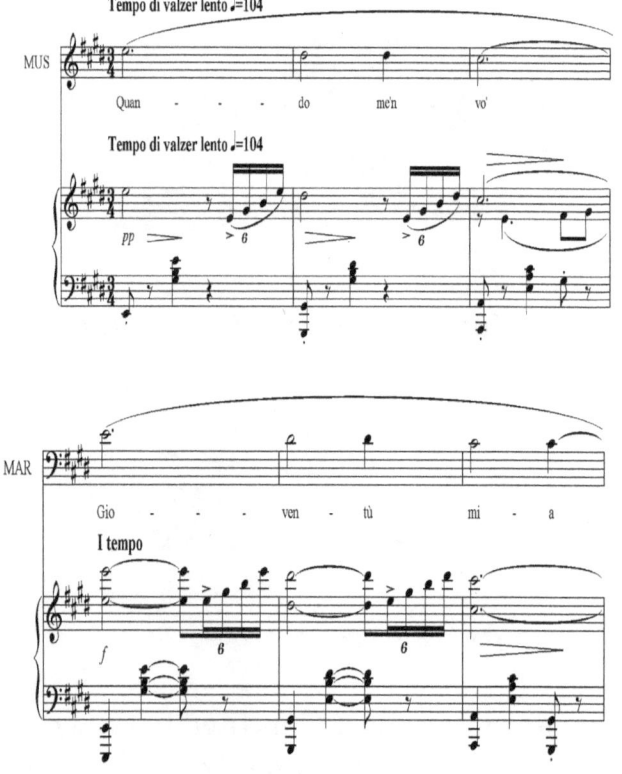

It is introduced on-stage a French retreat beginning with the music coming from the left flats. In the *coda*, at the tempo set by the band, the previous episodes are added. This strategy of reminiscence has a dramatic purpose since Puccini does not portray evolving characters but a reality, the bohemian life, in which love is only a break and time is an elusive abstraction passing inexorably.

Scene III

It is interesting to notice how Mimì, after her entry at the *barriera d'Enfer* (Scene III), worn by the progress of the illness, in the second bar, second triplet, proposes again the word *'scusi'* as in her first entry of the first scene.

On this occasion too, the conversational tone of Mimì is mainly tuned on the A in the second space of the treble staff. The information the maid asks a soldier about Marcello is in spoken tone, with an intermediate-low intonation structured in a descending direction, above all in semitones and short intervals:

While the bells of the Maria Teresa hostel ring for Matins, the motif of *La Bohème* precedes the arrival of Marcello:

✓ Duet Mimì and Marcello

The duet of Mimì and Marcello is dominated by the hurt of the protagonist who has lost her Rodolfo; this is followed by the frantic demand for help and the description of the poet's behavior. Speaking to Marcello about Rodolfo, though at a different pitch, some figures that appeared in the first scene to introduce the poet are now proposed again.
Let's consider the following examples:

These musical devices probably have the function to refer to the poet's spirit, already expressed in the first scene. The tone of Marcello's response is a mixture of sympathy and admonishment; the tone is conversational again when he describes how Rodolfo joined him in the dead of night.

✓ Rodolfo returns onstage

Rodolfo, woken up, is about to go out of the Cabaret, searching for Marcello; his entry onstage is introduced by the motif *Nei cieli bigi*. A new motif of the tenor is proposed in *Già un'altra volta credetti morto il mio cor* [Once, I believed my heart was dead forever], when he confides his intention to leave Mimì.

The tone is fluid, according to the metronome mark *Allegro moderato*, up to the two bars shown in couple of duplets, where there is the *'con dolore'* [with grief] specification in correspondence to the words *'per sempre'* [forever]:

In the second part, when Rodolfo lists the "faults" of Mimì, the tone becomes more dramatic and the suffering prevails, up to the confession of the truth: his Mimì is sick, so sick.

In these pages the tragedy is expressed mainly with the contrasts of the various sections. First and foremost the outburst of passion through which Rodolfo talks about his love:

The poet then sings of his fear, supported by the orchestra; it follows a melodic disheartening flattening in the phrase *Mimì è tanto malata* [Mimì is so very ill]:

The melody of the orchestra comes back to support the anguish of Rodolfo who admits his impotence before the gravity of the disease.

Soon after the expressive feeling of sadness and fear shifts to the profound waste of extreme poverty *La mia stanza è una tana squallida...* [My room is a squalid den...]. Rodolfo lacks a comfortable abode, a fire heating it up, and his love does not return medicine and doctors for his Mimì. Perhaps his love kills her: the poet's heart is worn out by regret. The whole profound hurt of the feeling is mirrored in the melody which grieves with its characters.

✓ *DONDE LIETA USCÌ* [From whence she joyously left]

The cough and strong sobs reveal the presence of Mimì. Rodolfo, after the initial wonder of seeing his beloved, cuddles her. To the noisy laughs of Musetta, coming from the Cabaret, Marcello goes off-stage re-entering *impetuosamente* [impetuously], accompanied by a comic passage about the infidelity of his belle.
Once alone with Rodolfo, Mimì starts to sing *Donde lieta uscì*. The orchestra proposes again some of the motifs already heard in the previous scenes. It is important to notice that the first bars of the piece retrace the music structure of the inception of *Mi chiamano Mimì*:

Again, in the bars corresponding to *a intesser finti fior!* [to embroider make-believe flowers!], there are some thematic references (*non vado sempre a Messa* [I don't often go to church]), to the first aria:

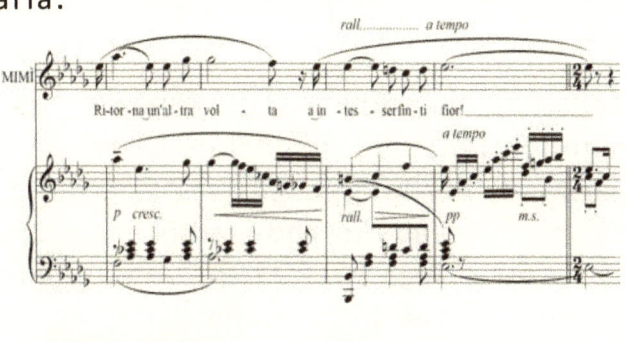

The same melody comes back one more time to name the things left at home: the golden hairband, the books of prayers, to be wrapped up in an apron.

Recalling the pink bonnet, Puccini has highlighted the importance of this garment, marking it with its own melody that, already introduced in the Latin Quarter, comes back at the time of the farewell in the third scene.

The following lines *Bada, sotto il guanciale c'è la cuffietta rosa* [Look, under the pillow you'll find the pink bonnet] recall the motif of Scene II *Andiam per la cuffietta?* [Shall we get the bonnet?]:

Among the numerous elements present over the opera, the pink bonnet is without a doubt the most important because it symbolizes the time of happiness, of love and the carefreeness that no longer will return. From this moment on the bonnet, and with it the emotion generated through its recollection, is rubbed into the spectator's memory. Its value, over the dramatic development, is embellished so much that it becomes a metaphor: in the second scene it can be interpreted as the launch of happiness and love; in the third scene it is seen as the object of memory, recalling the past time, of experienced love; in the fourth scene, it will be placed in Rodolfo's heart, like an emblematic seal that is born from the bosom and to which it returns to rest, until the last journey.

The whole piece is written prevalently in a low-key tone, reaching an oasis of lyrical effusion in the final section *Se vuoi, serbarla a ricordo d'amor!* [If you want to, keep it as a souvenir of our love!]:

✓ ADDIO DOLCE SVEGLIARE [Goodbye, sweet awakening]

Upon an intensely lyrical melody the duet between Mimì and Rodolfo *Addio dolce svegliare* originates; it is inspired by the song *Sole e amore* [Sun and love] written by Puccini in 1888 for the review «Paganini».

The passionate duet goes on until the noise of broken dishes and glasses, coming from the inside of the Cabaret, announces the wrangle between Marcello and Musetta who bursts running into the scene, followed by her lover. The return of Musetta and Marcello changes this section into a quartet, with the amazing contrast of the glow rally of these two characters and the love idyll of Mimì and Rodolfo. The four voices join together in the same melody only some bars before the end, even presenting the voices of the two sopranos at the unison and the tenor at the octave:

While Mimì and Rodolfo decide to wait for Spring to break them up, Musetta and Marcello say, rather - yell out, *Addio* [farewell] in a prosy and declaimed style in correspondence to the exclamations *Pittore da bottega! Vipera! Rospo! Strega!* [housepainter! Viper! Toad! Witch!], to convey with a bigger truth the importance of the quarrel:

Soon after, the music recalls the love spirit while Mimì and Rodolfo's voices recur on the motif of *La Bohème*, to strengthen the ideal of love, youth, the carefree poverty, the hand-to-mouth existence.

Quadro IV
The IV and last scene opens, under the melodic point of view, as the first one:

Scenically too it is proposed again in the same cold attic; it almost seems like a repetition of the first scene, except that the orchestra which plays up the timbre of instruments in order to convey the time continuity of the action.

This scene is dominated by the melancholy concealed under the nuance of a fake cheerfulness, which at some points is exasperated to disguise the profound inner turmoil.

Rodolfo and Marcello try to work but are not able to focus their attention since they are fascinated by the memory of their respective lovers, evoked by the relative melodies.

When they restart working, the motif of the first scene, when Rodolfo is alone, before Mimì enters, is introduced.

When Rodolfo and Marcello throw the pen and the brush respectively, the orchestra again plays the theme of *Fremon già nell'anima le dolcezze estreme* [Already I taste in spirit the heights of tenderness]:

Hence the duet between Rodolfo and Marcello originates in: *O Mimì tu più non torni* [O Mimi, you will return no more], *O Mimì mia breve gioventù* [Oh! Mimì, how brief my youth was], *Ah! Vien sul mio cuor poiché è morto amor* [Come to my heart, to my broken heart, oh, come to my heart, for love is dead]. At the end, as in Scene I, Schaunard returns, accompanied by his motif, together with Colline. Puccini aimed to insert at this point, another group scene recreating a cheerful atmosphere having the function to render a bigger contrast with the final next scene of the death. This time though, the lunch consisted of only a herring. In order not to think and focus too much on the material needs, the starvation and the coldness – that poverty cannot satisfy – the four friends have nothing to do but to play around, improvise a cheerful put-on; structurally it calls for a sequence of dances: gavotte, fandango and a square dance for Rodolfo and Marcello, ending with a duel between Schaunard and Colline. Note how in this cheerful duel some tools of the fireplace are used to highlight their futility, since the fire is out.

On the high-spirited music in the key of B flat major, well describing this context, a dark chord of E minor in tritone relation, realized in tremolo by the whole orchestra, suddenly falls to damp down the action. This is the moment when Musetta, deeply dismayed, bursts into the scene opening wide the door:

Mimì returns to die close to her Rodolfo. She enters the scene accompanied by her motif. Note, yet, that the structure of the *Leitmotiv* of the protagonist, when she was in the attic, differs from Scene I for tonality and for the repetition of the theme in descending tones:

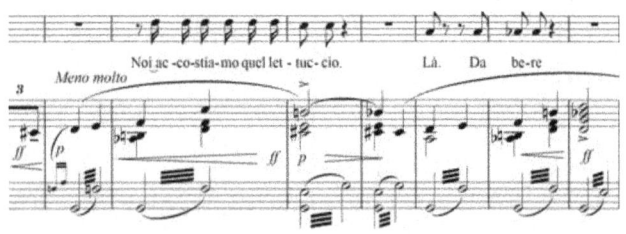

It is as if the melodic line and the accompaniment would describe the disease revealing the inexorability of its course. This melody proceeds up till Mimì is laid on the bed.

During Musetta's story the music reports the theme of Mimì's aria, in Scene I. Note how the melody of the words *Dove stia? Cerca, Cerca...* [I didn't know where she was living, so I searched, and searched...] corresponds to the one of the phrases *Mi piaccion quelle cose* [My story is brief. I delight in these pleasures] and *Germoglia in un vaso una rosa* [A rose blossoms in my vase]:

Later, the excruciating impulse of Mimì *Ancor sento la vita qui* [I feel life again here] recalls the love melody:

✓ VECCHIA ZIMARRA [DEAR OLD COAT]

A new motif summing up the variety of feelings of the *bohemians* is Colline's aria, *Vecchia zimarra*.

Technically this piece does not present any particular difficulty, but requires deep interpretative skills; the old coat is the symbol of pity and all the emotions are present in the finale section of the opera (*Vecchia zimarra, senti, io resto al pian, tua scendere il sacro monte or devi* [Dear old coat, listen, I stay here below, but you must now ascend the mount of piety!]).

Time itself is a parody of the farewell to Mimì who herself is the symbol of youth and serenity. It is very clear how these lines show the cause of happiness amidst poverty as well as pure misery, whose richness lies in one's own dignity (*Mai curvasti il logoro dorso ai ricchi e dai potenti* [You never bent your threadbare back to the rich and powerful]). The public too shares this farewell since it attended the purchase of the old garment[15] and its multiple uses, as cold repair and ample cover for the much loved books. Again, in Colline's words there is the unvoiced reference to the carefree and gleeful youth of the *bohèmiens* (*Passar nelle tue tasche come in antri tranquilli filosofi e poeti* [You have sheltered in your pockets like peaceful caves, philosophers and poets]). Now that Mimì is dying, and everything which is a metaphor with her, just the last word needs to be ut-

---

[15] Musetta too decides to pawn her earrings to scrape together some penny in order to purchase some medicine and to let a doctor come. But, beyond the endearment of the woman, these jewels do not entail an emotional involvement, because they do not contain themselves an affective and symbolic value like Colline's old coat. So, they are not part of the past, the story and the life of the *bohèmiens*.

tered: *addio* (*Ora che I giorni lieti fuggir, ti dico addio o fedele amico mio, addio, addio* [Now that happy days have fled, I bid you farewell, my faithful friend, farewell, farewell]).

The score reports: [Colline] «He puts the bundle under his arm, then whispers to Schaunard: "Schaunard, each separately, let's combine two kindly acts; mine is this [*indicating his overcoat*]... and you... [*pointing to Mimì and Rodolfo*] leave the two of them alone».

✓ SONO ANDATI? FINGEVO DI DORMIRE... [HAVE THEY GONE? I PRETENDED TO BE ASLEEP]

Once the *bohèmiens* are out of the room, Mimì and Rodolfo are alone at last and the orchestra renews the love theme:

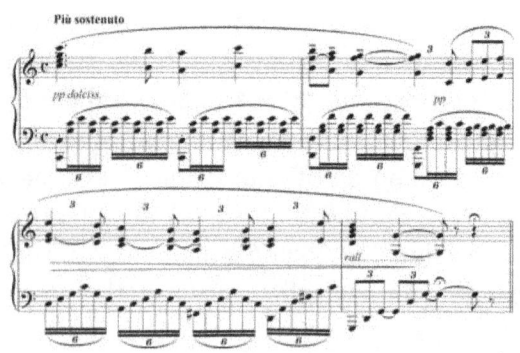

Soon thereafter, Mimì sings her last song: a harrowing melody in C minor, the last new theme of the opera. In each bar, on the downbeat the melody descends degree by degree, as if it accompanies the declining strength of the protagonist. At the end of this sequence Mimì gathers herself together and, as specified in the score, "getting up a little on the bed", swells her last life beats in the lyric and distressing phrase *Sei il mio amore e tutta la mia vita* [You are my love and my whole life] which makes an end of her stamina, directing her to death.

There is nothing left for it now except time to recall the journey of the sweet memory. *Bella come un tramonto* [Beautiful as the dawn] describes vividly the image of the end, and the only way to survive to last moments, is the memory of the lovely past.

The retake of the theme *Mi chiamano Mimì* [Yes, they call me Mimì] is reaffirmed twice, in descending movement; the pauses between '*il perché*' and '*non so*' [I don't know why] are of a double value compared to those ones of the first scene, as there is quaver rest between '*non*' and '*so*':

Rodolfo, as specified in the score, "takes the bonnet from its place over his heart and hands it out to Mimì". Thrilled to see her bonnet again (and with Mimì the spectator too), she recalls their first encounter, in the attic; musically the theme *Sventata, la chiave della stanza dove l'ho lasciata?* [Oh! foolish me! Where have I left the key to my room?] is proposed again:

"In a weak voice she repeats Rodolfo's words" and starts to sing *Che gelida manina* [How cold your little hand is]. Soon after she "has a sudden spasm of coughing, she falls back with exhaustion".
Schaunard, Marcello and Musetta return; Musetta hands out the muff to Mimì, who takes it 'with an almost childish joy'. Deeming it was Rodolfo's present (also for the sudden intervention of Musetta, that in this case discloses her kindness, until then over-

shadowed by her affected personality), Mimì, despite her condition is still able to be worried about the gift she received - too expensive for the poets' condition.

She thanks him with intense tenderness and would like to comfort him: *Sto bene... Pianger così perché?* [I'm fine... Why are you crying like this?]

Here the human side of Mimì ends; from the next bar her voice is faint, the words are spaced out by rests, the music is discrete, structured by dynamic marks going from *pppp* to *rall.* and *morendo sempre*. It then comes to her leaving 'in a weak voice, more and more fainting': *Qui amor... sempre con te!.. Le mani... al caldo... e......dormire...* [I'm here... my love,... always with you! My hands... in the warm... and... to sleep...].

After the last word of Mimì, '*dormire*', the music too stops (long rest); she gives the last sigh: the music dies with Mimì.

The last section provides for Musetta's prayer, by now useless, as well as the valueless distress of Rodolfo. Schaunard, instead, realizes that Mimì has died, and communicates it to Marcello. Rodolfo does not understand right away what has just happened, but when he becomes aware of it he is carried away by dismay. With a voice choked with panic and emotion, he says: «What does it mean all this coming and going. Why are you staring at me?...».

The *pathos* is mainly expressed by the pedal point on A, held by a clarinet and a double-bass:

It follows the full-power attack of Mimì's threnody and the last high G sharp of Rodolfo, which "dashes to Mimi's bedside, scoops her up in his arms crying out in extreme desperation".

The torment is on the summit: Rodolfo, crying, "throws himself on Mimì's lifeless body".

The opera ends with the same chord progression of *Vecchia zimarra* sung by Colline (I – VII – VI – VII - I).

An effective and poignant way to say farewell through music, recalling their first, emotional and passionate meeting as the philosopher offers some last minutes of warmth by covering her with his old coat.

Such repeal strengthens the perception of death as a metaphor of the conclusion of a period of existence, and the suggestive exit from a world made by things, which die with Mimì.

BIBLIOGRAPHY

- ADAMI GIUSEPPE, *Il romanzo della vita di Giacomo Puccini*, Milan–Rome: Rizzoli, 1944
- AMY DOMINIQUE, *Giacomo Puccini. L'homme et son oeuvre*, Paris: Seghers, 1970
- ARNESEN IRIS J., *The Romantic World of Puccini: A New Critical Appraisal of the Operas*, Jefferson, NC: McFarland, 2009
- ARRIGHI GINO, *La corrispondenza di Giacomo Puccini con Maria Bianca Ginori Lisci*, in *Critica pucciniana*, Lucca: La Nuova Grafica Lucchese, 1976
- ATLAS ALLAN W., *Multivalence, Ambiguity and Non-ambiguity: Puccini and the Polemicists*, «Journal of the Royal Musical Association», CXVIII, 1993
- BARAGWANATH NICHOLAS, *The Musical Style of Giacomo Puccini*, London: Ashgate, 2008
- BARESEL ALFRED, *Giacomo Puccini. Leben und Werk*, Hamburg: Sikorski, 1954
- BARILLI BRUNO, *Il paese del melodramma*, Milan: Adelphi, 2000
- BEGHELLI MARCO, *Quel «Lago di Massaciuccoli tanto... povero d'ispirazione!»*.

D'Annunzio-Puccini, lettere di un accordo mai nato, «Nuova rivista musicale italiana», XX, 1986
- BERNARDONI VIRGILIO, *Giacosa librettista per Puccini nello specchio della genesi di «Bohème»*, in *Giuseppe Giacosa e le seduzioni della scena. Tra teatro e opera lirica*, edited by Roberto Alonge, Bari: Edizioni di Pagina, 2007
- BERNARDONI VIRGILIO, *Verso Bohème. Gli abbozzi del libretto negli archivi di Giuseppe Giacosa e Luigi Illica*, Florence: Olschki, 2008 («Centro studi Giacomo Puccini, Testi e documenti», 1).
- BIANCHI MICHELE, *La poetica di Giacomo Puccini: sull'arte e nell'arte di un drammaturgo*, Pisa: ETS, 2001
- BONACCORSI ALFREDO, *Giacomo Puccini e i suoi antenati musicali*, Milan: Curci, 1950
- BONAVENTURA ARNALDO, *Giacomo Puccini. L'uomo – l'artista (profilo)*, Livorno: Giusti, 1925
- BUDDEN JULIAN, *Puccini. His Life and Works*, Oxford-New York: Oxford University Press, 2002

— *Puccini's Transpositions*, «Studi pucciniani», 1, 1998

- CASINI CLAUDIO, *Giacomo Puccini*, Turin UTET, 1978
- CHRISTEN NORBERT, *Giacomo Puccini. Analytische Untersuchungen der Melodik, Harmonik und Instrumentation*, Hamburg: Wagner, 1978
- CLAUSSE ELEONORE, *Puccini*, Madrid: Espasa–Calpe, 1980
- CORSE SANDRA, *«Mi chiamano Mimì»: The Role of Women in Puccini's Operas*, «The Opera Quarterly», I/1, 1983
- CRESTI RENZO, *Giacomo Puccini e il Postmoderno. Vita e opere viste in una nuova prospettiva*, Fucecchio: Edizione dell'Elba, 2007
    — *Giacomo Puccini. Lucca and its Musicians, the Works of the most performed Composer in the World and their Operatic Context*, Lucca: Maria Pacini Fazzi, 1998
- *Critica pucciniana*, Lucca: La Nuova Grafica Lucchese, 1976
- D.E.U.M.M. (Dizionario Enciclopedico della Musica e dei Musicisti), Turin: UTET, 1985
- D'AMBRA LUCIO, *Puccini*, Rome: Colombo, 1940
- D'AMICO FEDELE, *L'albero del bene e del male. Naturalismo e decadentismo in Puccini*,

a cura di Jacopo Pellegrini, Lucca: Maria Pacini Fazzi, 2000
   —*Naturalismo e decadentismo in Puccini*, in *I casi della musica*, Milan: Il Saggiatore, 1962
- DAHLHAUS CARL, *Drammaturgia dell'opera italiana*, in *Storia dell'opera italiana*, edited by Lorenzo Bianconi and Giorgio Pestelli, VI, *Teorie e tecniche. Immagini e fantasmi*, Turin: EDT/Musica, 1988
   —*Estetica della musica*, Rome: Astrolabio, 2009
- DAVIS SHELBY, *David Belasco and Giacomo Puccini: Their Collaborations*, in *Opera and the Golden West. The Past, Present, and Future of Opera in the U.S.A.*, edited by J. L. Di Gaetani and J. Sirefman, Rutherford–London: Farleigh Dickinson University Press–Associated University Presses, 1994
- DE RANIERI ORIANO, LUBRANI MAURO, *Giacomo Puccini: luoghi e sentimenti*, Florence: Polistampa, 2008
- DEAN WINTON, *Puccini*, in *The Heritage of Music*, edited by H. Foss, III, London: Oxford University Press, 1951,
- DELLA SETA FABRIZIO, *«... non senza pazzia». Prospettive sul teatro musicale*, Rome: Carocci, 2008

— *Italia e Francia nell'Ottocento*, vol. 9, Turin: EDT, 1993
- DEMEL STEFAN, DEMEL GERNOT, *Giacomo Puccini: Eine Psychobiographie*, Stuttgart: Kohlhammer, 1995
- DI GAETANI JOHN LOUIS, *Puccini the Thinker. The Composer's Intellectual and Dramatical Development*, New York–Bern–Frankfurt: Peter Lang, 1987
- *Esotismo e colore locale nell'opera di Puccini. Atti del I Convegno internazionale sull'opera di Puccini* (Torre del Lago, 1983), edited by J. Maehder, Pisa: Giardini, 1985
- FAJTH TIBOR, NÁDOR TÁMÁS, *Puccini*, Budapest: Gondolat, 1977
- FELLERER KARL GUSTAV, *Giacomo Puccini*, Potsdam: Athenaion, 1937
- FRACCAROLI ARNALDO, *La vita di Giacomo Puccini*, Milan: Ricordi, 1957
- GALLINI NATALE, *Gli anni giovanili di Giacomo Puccini*, «L'approdo musicale», II/6, 1959

—*Puccini. Documenti*, «La Scala», V/60, 1954
- GATTI GUIDO M., *Rileggendo le opere di Giacomo Puccini*, in *Giacomo Puccini*, edited by C. Sartori, Milan: Ricordi, 1959

- GAUTHIER ANDRE, *Puccini*, Paris: Éditions du Seuil, 1976
- GERHARD ANSELM, *The Urbanization of Opera. Music Theater in Paris in the Nineteenth Century*, Chicago: The University of Chicago Press, 1998
- GHERARDI LUCIANO, *Appunti per una lettura delle varianti nelle opere di Giacomo Puccini*, «Studi musicali», VI, 1977
- *Giacomo Puccini nel centenario della nascita*, «Lucca. Rassegna del Comune», II/4, 1958
- *Giacomo Puccini*, edited by C. Sartori, Milan: Ricordi, 1959
- *Giacomo Puccini. L'uomo, il musicista, il panorama europeo, Atti del Convegno internazionale di studi su Giacomo Puccini nel 70° anniversario della morte* (Lucca, 25-29 novembre 1994), edited by G. Biagi Ravenni and C. Gianturco, Lucca: LIM, 1997
- GILLIO PIER GIUSEPPE, *Il proto-libretto di «Bohème»: materiali preparatori nell'archivio di Casa Giacosa*, «Nuova rivista musicale italiana», XXXI, 1997
- GIRARDI MICHELE, *Puccini: His International Art*, Chicago: The University of Chicago Press, 2002
- GIUDICI ELVIO, *Puccini*, Milan: Ricordi, 1994

- GREENFELD HOWARD, *Puccini. A Biography*, London: Robert Hale, 1981
  —*Puccini: Keeper of the Seal*, London: Arrow Books, 1958
- GUARNIERI CORAZZOL ADRIANA, *Opera e verismo: regressione del punto di vista e artificio dello straniamento*, in *Ruggero Leoncavallo nel suo tempo*, edited by J. Maehder and L. Guiot, Milan: Sonzogno, 1993
- HAYLOCK JULIAN, *Puccini: His Life and Music*, Naperville, Illinois: Sourcebooks Media Fusion, 2008
- HUGHES SPIKE, *Famous Puccini Operas: An Analytical Guide for the Opera-Goer and Armchair Listener*, New York: Dover, 1972
- KELKEL MANFRED, *Naturalisme, vérisme et réalisme dans l'opéra de 1890 à 1930*, Paris: Vrin, 1984
- KLONOVSKY MCHAEL, *Der Schmerz Der Schönheit: Über Giacomo Puccini*, Berlin: Berlin Verlag, 2008
- KRAUSSER HELMUT, *Die Jagdnach Corinna: eine Puccini-Recherche*, Munich: Belleville, 2008
- *Le Garzantine – Musica*, Milan: Garzanti Editore, 1996
- MACDONALD RAY S., *Puccini, King of Verismo*, New York: Vantage, 1973

- Magri Giorgio, *L'uomo Puccini*, Milan: Mursia, 1992
- Marchesi Gustavo, Di Gregorio Casati Marisa, *Puccini: Vissi d'arte, vissi d'amore: vita, immagini, ritratti*, Parma: Grafiche Step, 2003
- Mariani Renato, *Giacomo Puccini*, Turin: Arione, 1938
- Marnat Marcel, *Puccini*, Paris, Fayard, 2005
- Marotti Guido, *Valori concreti dell'arte pucciniana*, Viareggio: Bertolozzi, 1936
- Martínez Orlando, *El sentido humano en la obra de Puccini*, Buenos Aires: Ricordi Americana, 1958
- Martino Daniele A., *L'idillio imperfetto. Sentimenti ed eroine nei libretti per Puccini*, in *Teoria e storia dei generi letterari. La letteratura in scena. Il teatro del Novecento*, edited by G. Barberi Squarotti, Turin: Tirrenia, 1985
- Martinotti Sergio, «*Torna ai felici dì...*»: *il librettista Fontana*, in «Quaderni pucciniani», 3, 1992

    —*I travagliati Avant-Propos di Puccini*, in *Il melodramma italiano dell'Ottocento. Studi e ricerche per*

Massimo Mila, edited by G. Pestelli, Turin: Einaudi, 1977
- MEYEROWITZ JAN, *Puccini: Musica a doppio fondo*, «Nuova rivista musicale italiana», X, 1976
- MONALDI GINO, *Giacomo Puccini e la sua opera*, Rome: Mantegazza, 1924
- MORIN LABRECQUE ALBERTINE, *Puccini et ses opéras*, 1858-1924, Montréal: Éditions de l'Étoile, 1945
- MUSCO GIANFRANCO, *Musica e teatro in Giacomo Puccini*, vol. I, Cortona: Calosci, 1989
- *Musica e testo in Puccini*, Quaderni della Fondazione Festival pucciniano, 1, Pisa: Edizioni ETS, 1994
- NARDI PIERO, *Vita e tempo di Giuseppe Giacosa*, Milan: Mondadori, 1949
    — *«La bohème»: Opera in quattro atti (cinque quadri). L'atto denominato «Il cortile della casa di via Labruyère 8» di Illica e Giacosa*, «La Scala», IX/109, 1958
- NEISSER ARTHUR, *Giacomo Puccini. Sein Leben und sein Werk*, Leipzig: Reclam, 1928
- NEWMAN EARNEST, *Stories of the Great Operas*. Philadelphia: The Blakinson Company, 1930

- Oliván Federico, *Puccini. Su vida y su obra*, Madrid: Uguina, 1949
- Osborne Charles, *The Complete Operas of Puccini. A Critical Guide*, London: Gollancz, 1990
- Padellaro Laura, Dall'Ongaro, Michele, *Puccini. Tutte le opere*, Florence: Banca Toscana, 1989
- Paduano Guido, «*Come è difficile esser felici*». *Amore e amori nel teatro di Puccini*, Pisa: ETS, 2004
- Paladini Carlo, *Giacomo Puccini con l'epistolario inedito*, edited by M. Paladini, Firenze: Vallecchi, 1961
- Parker D. C., *A View of Giacomo Puccini*, «The Musical Quarterly», III, 1917
- Pernye András, *Giacomo Puccini*, Budapest: Gondolat, 1959
- Peyser Herbert F., *Puccini in Perspective*, «Musician», XXX/1, 1925
- Phillips-Matz Mary Jane, *Puccini: A Biography*, Boston: Northeastern University Press, 2002
- Pinzauti Leonardo, *Giacomo Puccini*, Turin: ERI, 1975
- Powers Harold S., *One Half-Step at a Time: Tonal Transposition and «Split Associa-*

tion» in Italian Opera, «Cambridge Opera Journal», VII, 1995
- *Puccini*, edited by V. Bernardoni, Bologna: Il Mulino, 1996
- RAMSDEN TIMOTHY, *Puccini and His Operas*, Staplehurst: Spellmount, 1996
- RESCIGNO EDUARDO, *Dizionario pucciniano: le opere, i cantanti, i personaggi, i direttori d'orchestra, gli scenografi, i librettisti, le fonti letterarie, i parenti, gli amici, le donne, le case, i viaggi, le automobili, la caccia, il cinematografo, i progetti*, Milan: Ricordi, 2004
- RICCI LUIGI, *Puccini interprete di se stesso*, Milan: Ricordi, 2003
- ROCCATAGLIATI ALESSANDRO, *La prefigurazione librettistica fra tardo Ottocento e "fine del melodramma": spigolature sui processi di modificazione*, in *L'opera prima dell'opera. Fonti, libretti, intertestualità*, edited by Alessandro Grilli, Pisa: PLUS, 2006
- ROSS PETER, SCHWENDIMANN-BERRA DONATA, *Sette lettere di Puccini a Giulio Ricordi*, «Nuova rivista musicale italiana», XIII, 1979

- RUBBOLI DANIELE, *Giacomo Puccini. L'ultimo di una «bottega» di musicisti*, Lucca: Maria Pacini Fazzi, 1990
- SANGUINETTI GIORGIO, *Puccini's Music in Italian Theoretical Literature of Its Day*, in *Tosca's Prism: Three Moments of Western Cultural History*, edited by Deborah Burton, Susan Vandiver Nicassio, Agostino Ziino, Boston: Northeastern University Press, 2004
- SANTI PIERO, *Senso comune e vocalità nel melodramma pucciniano*, «La rassegna musicale», XXVIII, 1958
- SARTI ADOLFO, *Puccini e le donne. Poesia e amore di donne nelle opere di Giacomo Puccini*, Rome: Ruffolo, 1950
- SARTI EMILIANO, *Giacomo Puccini. Vita e opere*, Lucca: Maria Pacini Fazzi, 2007
- SARTORI CLAUDIO, *Puccini*, Milan: Nuova Accademia, 1978
- SCHICKLING DIETER, *Giacomo Puccini: la vita e l'arte*, Ghezzano: Felici, 2008
- SEIFERT WOLFGANG, *Giacomo Puccini*, Leipzig: Breitkopf und Härtel, 1957
- SICILIANO ENZO, *Puccini*, Milan: Rizzoli, 1976
- SOUTHWELL-SANDER PETER, *Puccini*, London–New York: Omnibus Press, 1996

- STENZL JÜRG, *Von Giacomo Puccini zu Luigi Nono. Italienische Musik 1922-1952. Faschismus – Resistenza – Republik*, Buren: Knuf, 1990
- TAROZZI GIUSEPPE, *L'amore cattivo. Vita di Giacomo Puccini*, Milan: Camunia, 1988
    — *Puccini*, New York: Treves, 1985
    — *Puccini. La fine del bel canto*, Milan: Bompiani, 1972
- TERENZIO VINCENZO, *Ritratto di Puccini*, Bergamo: Conti, 1954
- *The Puccini Companion*, edited by S. Puccini and W. Weaver, New York-London: Norton, 1994
- THIESS FRANK, *Puccini. Versucheiner Psychologie seiner Musik*, Hamburg: Krüger, 1947
- TITONE ANTONINO, *Puccini*, Treviso: Matteo, 1994
    —*Vissi d'arte. Puccini e il disfacimento del melodramma*, Milan: Feltrinelli, 1972
- VALLERONI ALDO, *Puccini minimo*, Ivrea: Priuli & Verlucca, 1983
- VAUGHAN DENIS, *Puccini's Orchestration*, «Proceedings of the Royal Musical Association», LXXXVII, 1960-61

- WEAVER WILLIAM, *Puccini: The Man and His Music*, New York: Metropolitan Opera Guild, 1978
    — *The Golden Century of Italian Opera. From Rossini to Puccini*, London–New York: Thames & Hudson, 1988
- WEISSMANN ADOLF, *Giacomo Puccini*, München: Drei Masken, 1922.
- WILSON ALEXANDRA, *The Puccini Problem. Opera, Nationalism and Modernity*, Cambridge: Cambridge University Press, 2006
    — *Torrefranca vs. Puccini: Embodying a Decadent Italy*, «Cambridge Opera Journal», XIII/1, 2001
- WILSON CONRAD, *Giacomo Puccini*, London: Phaidon, 1997
- ZAFRED MARIO, *L'orchestra nelle opere di Puccini*, «Musica d'oggi», II, 1959
- ZONDERGELD REIN A., *Ornament und Emphase. Illica, d'Annunzio und der Symbolismus*, in *Oper und Operntext*, edited by J. Malte Fischer, Heidelberg: Winter, 1985

www.ingramcontent.com/pod-product-compliance
Lightning Source LLC
Chambersburg PA
CBHW022116090426
42743CB00008B/872